AF521686

In recognition of our 100th anniversary, the Washington Wellesley Club is proud to sponsor the publication of this book.

We dedicate this volume to all alumnae and friends of Wellesley College, past, present, and future. We hope the images in this book will both introduce new friends to the beauty and spirit of Wellesley, and enable alumnae everywhere to rekindle memories of their years at this very special place.

The Washington Wellesley Club, 1988

It is a landscape not merely beautiful, but with a marked individual character not represented so far as I know on the ground of any other college in the country.

Frederick Law Olmsted, Jr. in letter to President Hazard, 1902

You have chosen a place eternally beautiful.

William Butler Yeats to Mrs. Durant

WELLESLEY COLLEGE

INTRODUCTION BY ELISABETH GRIFFITH '69

PHOTOGRAPHED BY DAN DRY

HARMONY HOUSE
PUBLISHERS LOUISVILLE

Executive Editors: William Butler and William Strode
Library of Congress Catalog Number: 87- 083175
Hardcover International Standard Book Number: 0-916509-42-7
Printed in USA by Gateway Press, Louisville, Kentucky
First Edition printed Fall 1988 by Harmony House Publishers,
P.O. Box 90, Prospect, Kentucky 40059 (502)228-2010 / 228-4446
Copyright © 1988 by Harmony House Publishers
Photographs copyright © 1988 Dan Dry
Additional photography by Gustave Freedman
on page 72, and by Mark Lennihan on pages 86-87

This book or portions thereof may not be reproduced in any form without permission of Harmony House Publishers. Photographs may not be reproduced in any form without permission of Dan Dry or the photographers cited above.

The publishers wish to thank the following for their help and hospitality during the production year of this book: Barbara Schwartz Garlock of the Washington Wellesley Club; Nancy Agnew, Vice President of Public Affairs for Wellesley College; Anne M. Morgan, Executive Director of the Alumnae Association; Wilma R. Slaight, Wellesley College Archivist; Marjorie Halperin, Director for Clubs; and Romi Cummings, Director of Publications for Wellesley College. Thanks also go to Aviva Segal, Heidi Avery and *Wellesley* magazine.

Flower Sunday

REMEMBERING WELLESLEY: REFLECTION AND RESONANCE

By Elisabeth Griffith '69
Headmistress, The Madeira School, McLean, Virginia

Still and silent, the striking photographs in this book have stirred many memories of Wellesley for me. I look at them and I hear the Bach choir practicing; oars clicking in shells cutting across the lake; the crackle of dry leaves and the crunch of hard snow underfoot; tennis balls thudding; radiators clanging; telephones ringing; laughter and chatter drifting across a dormitory courtyard. I look at them and I recall the cool quiet angles of sunlight and shadow in the chapel; the smell of chalk dust, floor wax, and formaldehyde; the grainy touch of Gothic grey stone; the taste of peppermint ice cream with hot fudge sauce.

These images evoke a sense of the physical reality of the College — beautiful, serene, changing by season but unchanged in character. I feel rooted there, in the bedrock of an intellectual community of women, an environment which nurtured an independent sisterhood. Confidence in the capacity of women to undertake any challenge and succeed was pervasive. Freed from adolescent peer pressure to play dumb in the presence of boys, unfettered by society's assumptions about appropriate roles for the "second sex," Wellesley students could prove to themselves how competent each was. At Wellesley there was no doubt about the ability of women to accomplish anything they chose, so self-doubt was supplanted by self-confidence.

In intellectual rigor Wellesley remains the match of any male institution, as its founder intended and its faculty guaranteed. Balancing that academic emphasis is a sense of community and an environment in which individual gifts are nurtured. Long before educational psychologists like those at Wellesley's Center for Research on Women had established the need for women to balance "achievement" and "affiliation" (put plainly, work and love), Wellesley fostered that equilibrium.

I entered Wellesley in 1965, without benefit of recent studies which affirm that single sex colleges provide women with greater self-esteem and more leadership roles, factors which both enhance and predict future success in any field. I didn't know then that, as a group, women's college graduates would have more successful careers than women graduates of coeducational institutions, or that women's colleges inculcate values of cooperation, consensus building, and community service. All I knew was that the admissions officers and alumnae I met told me that Wellesley would make a difference in my life. And it did, in ways I never could have anticipated.

Terminal figure for "The Fountain of Man" by Charles Grafly — in the porte cochere of Tower Court

Coming from a large suburban high school in the midwest, where competition among girls for both grades and dates was cut-throat, I was astonished to find so little of that at Wellesley. There students were motivated to compete against themselves rather than each other. For four years I never knew anyone's standing, except when lists of Durant Scholars, Phi Beta Kappas , or honors candidates were published.

How we looked and dressed also seemed to matter less, except to strict housemothers or visiting moms, who seemed shocked by our scruffiness. We looked unkempt except on Fridays before weekends away. For many of us, Wellesley fostered female friendship and a strong sense of sisterhood.

I graduated from Wellesley at the end of the 1960's, the decade of civil rights activism, anti-war protests, the Beatles, Motown and miniskirts, the end of parietals and the beginning of the women's movement. After thriving in Wellesley's congenial climate, it was a shock to encounter sexism and skepticism within days of enrolling in graduate school. One male student demanded to know why I was taking the place of a more deserving man; one male professor required all female students to request permission to enter his seminar, since in his experience girls didn't speak up. All of this was an unfathomable situation to me. Within months I went from being a member of the majority to being a visible minority in a field where men were dominant.

My field is history, and even history was being written then as a masculine chronicle whose protagonists were exclusively male. As I pursued my doctorate, Women's Studies was just being established as a field. I began to learn about women who were not then part of any history curriculum; about women reformers, factory workers and field hands. Many among the most notable were Wellesley graduates, or alumnae of other women's colleges or of female institutions like the settlement houses or the suffrage movement.

I learned how difficult it had been for women to gain access to education in the era of Wellesley's founding. Such efforts had been undercut by accepted medical (masculine) authority which purported that studying Latin or algebra, indeed any thinking at all, would render women infertile as vital energy was diverted from the uterus to the brain. Labeling this theory as hokum was a lively mother of seven and a superior thinker, Elizabeth Cady Stanton. It was she who had had the audacity in 1848 to demand voting rights for women and who had set the agenda for the first women's movement in this country. Mrs. Stanton became my dissertation topic.

As a biographer, I searched for the formative events in her life, those incidents that make a difference to the outcome of each pilgrim's progress. Applying that same lens now to my own life, Wellesley's impact is easily identified. By presuming my inherent ability, by giving me opportunities to lead and to observe female leaders, by teaching me to value other women, Wellesley ignited a commitment to feminism and propelled me into the women's movement. At this stage in my life, I see that my politics, my philosophy, my professional choices and my private life reflect Wellesley's standard of female equality. I know that many other Wellesley women have found these same standards significant in their lives.

Like thousands who have preceded and followed me at Wellesley, I have enjoyed the company and profited from the experience and wisdom of Wellesley friends and mentors. It was a Wellesley woman who hired me for my first job, and another who recruited me for the women's movement. President Keohane might have been referring to my husband when she quoted the Wellesley spouse who declared, "My wife went to Wellesley, and she's never gotten over it!" Few of us do.

Now, after some years as an academic and an activist, I am about to become Headmistress of the Madeira School, a four-year girl's preparatory school in McLean, Virginia (founded by a Vassar graduate in 1906). I am eager to apply what I have learned about the education of women to the future needs of my students. I want those young women to be inspired and empowered by their experience in a single-sex setting.

The memories of sights, sounds, friends and feelings prompted by this book are sharper and more tangible than my recollection of chemical formulae, economic theories, or German conjugations. I cannot remember the words to the Alma Mater, but my perception of Wellesley and its importance in my life is vividly clear and keenly appreciated. I hope this book stimulates the memories of each alumna. We were all lucky to have had such an opportunity and such a unique and enduring experience in a very special place. I'm looking forward to turning these pages with my daughter Megan, in an early recruitment effort.

Houghton Memorial Chapel

A WELLESLEY CHRONOLOGY

Compiled by Wilma R. Slaight

1870 Wellesley Female Seminary chartered by the Commonwealth of Massachusetts

1873 Name changes to Wellesley College

1875 College opens on September 8 with 314 students. The President (Ada Howard) and almost all of the faculty are women

1877 Tradition of Tree Day begins; each class at Wellesley plants a class tree

1878 Schools of Music and Art open

1878 Students' Aid Society formed to assist students with college expenses

1879 First commencement; 18 students graduate

1880 Alumnae Association founded

1880 Preparatory department discontinued

1881 Henry Fowle Durant, founder of Wellesley College, dies

1882 Alice Freeman (age 27) becomes President

1886 Eliot becomes the first cooperative house (house where students could work to earn part of their fees)

1887 First black graduate, Harriet Rice

1888 Helen Shafer becomes President after Alice Freeman marries George Herbert Palmer, Professor of Philosophy at Harvard, (December 1887) and resigns; Miss Shafer promotes the first major curricular reform

1888-89 First foreign student, Kin Kato from Japan

1888 *The Courant*, the first of a succession of student newspapers, begins publication

1889 *Legenda*, the yearbook, begins publication

1891 Mary Whiton Calkins establishes one of first psychology laboratories in country at Wellesley

1894 Julie Irvine becomes President. She liberalizes some student rules, ends domestic work, makes chapel attendance voluntary

1894 First alumnae trustees elected to the Board of Trustees

1895 Tradition of hoop rolling begins

1895 "America the Beautiful" by Katharine Le Bates, Class of 1880 and member of the Depar ment of English Literature, is published

1896 Art and Music cease to be schools, become departments

1899 Caroline Hazard becomes President, and embarks on a building program to enhance Wellesley's facilities

1901 Student government association formed

1905 Phi Beta Kappa, Eta Chapter of Massach setts, installed at Wellesley

1911 Ellen Pendleton, Class of 1886, becomes President. Miss Pendleton serves longer than any other Wellesley President, 25 years

1914 College Hall burns, March 17

1917 Pauline Durant, cofounder of Wellesley College dies

922 Honors program begins

923 Alumnae Hall, the long-awaited student/ lumnae building opens

926 First junior year abroad (in 1980's Welle- ley greatly expands study abroad programs)

928 All students must take a general exam on heir major field of study

936 Mildred McAfee becomes President; Class of 1938 inaugurates a new tradition, unior Show (an original musical by members of the Junior Class)

938 Chapter of Sigma Xi Society installed at Vellesley

942-46 Mildred McAfee is given a leave of bsence from the College Presidency to lead he WAVES (Women's Reserve of U.S. Navy). While she is on leave the College is un by Marie Haffenreffer, senior alumnae rustee, Ella Keats Whiting, Dean of the College, and Lucy Wilson, Dean of Students

943 Washington Intership program begins (in the 1970's other internship opportunities are added); Four groups of the Navy Supply Corps live and train on campus

1945 Mildred McAfee receives the Distinguished Service Medal and marries Rev. Douglas Horton

1946 Emily Greene Balch, who taught economics and sociology 1896-1918, is awarded the Nobel Peace Prize

1949 Margaret Clapp, Pulitzer Prize-winning historian of the Class of 1930, becomes President

1950 Interdepartmental major first offered

1952 With the completion of the "new dorms," Bates, and Freeman, all students can be housed on campus--freshmen (and occasionally sophomores) no longer live in "the vil"

1958 Jewett Arts Center, designed by Paul Rudolph, opens

1966 Ruth Adams becomes President

1968 Curriculum revised to eliminate required English and Bible courses, and the general exam; Cross-registration program with M.I.T. begins. This was the first of a number of exchange arrangements available to students

1969 Continuing Education program begins

1970 Students may design their own majors

1971 Wellesley decides to remain single sex school

1972 Barbara Newell becomes President

1974 Center for Research on Women opens

1981 Nannerl Keohane, Class of 1961, becomes President

1981 Stone Center for Developmental Services and Studies opens

1983 Required writing program for Freshmen reinstated

1984 Interdisciplinary cluster program for first year students begins

Tower Court and Severance Hall

The conflict (over the site of Houghton Chapel) made manifest the vision of the college's landscape of Wellesley faculty women. They wanted it to embody elements of the English park, offering a feeling of unbounded space. They appreciated its rolling, sylvan beauty. While Cambridge critics snobbishly portrayed Wellesley as rural, Wellesley's women professors properly understood it as an English pastoral landscape in the manner of Capability Brown's aristocratic country houses.

Helen Lefkowitz Horowitz in *Alma Mater*, 1984

The glory of a beautiful campus, changing with the seasons, with the time to roam through it — let it seep into one's soul, as it were — can be a profoundly pleasurable, even a spiritual experience. My desk faces a wall today, but my memories include the whole pageant of New England's seasons. One reaches back into this as much as anything for recuperation and sustenance and sheer remembered joy during the course of a busy life.

Nayantara Pandit Sahgal '47 in *Wellesley After Images,* 1974

OLS
$\hat{\beta} = \frac{\sum(x_i-\bar{x})(y_i-\bar{y})}{\sum(y_i-\bar{y})^2}$
f(x)
Y
$y = \hat{\alpha} + \hat{\beta}X$
SCHEDULE
X

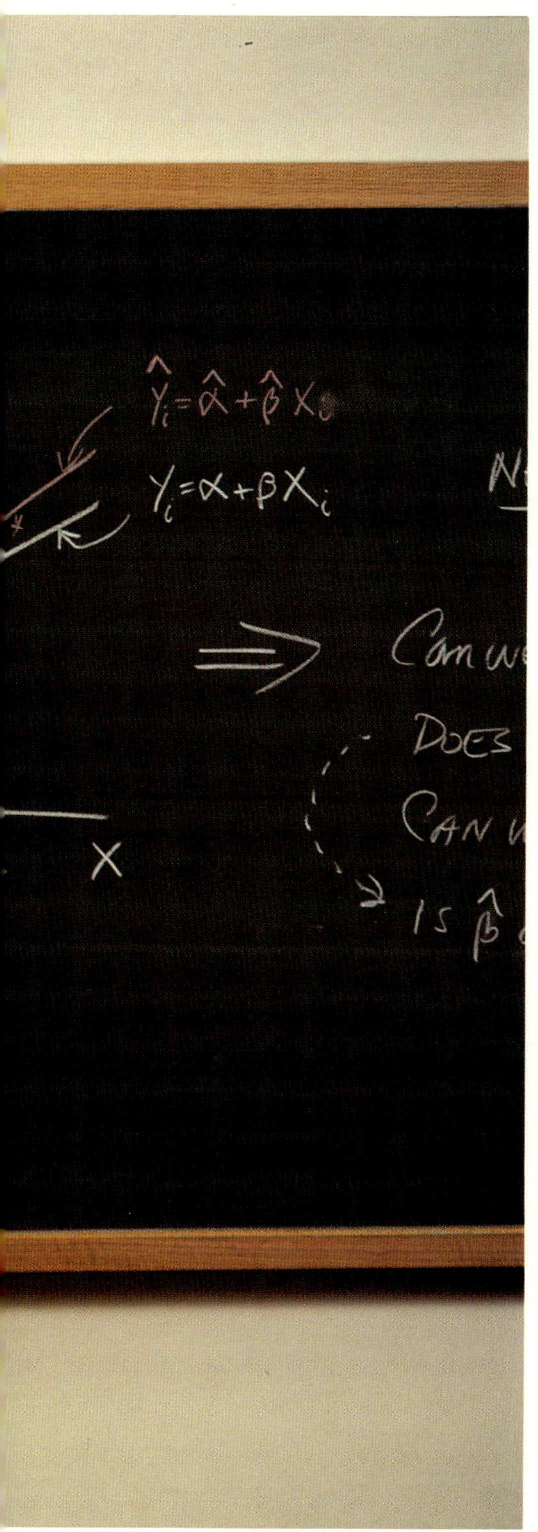

The most crucial single thing about Wellesley is its quality education. This is what has been the heart of Wellesley for almost a century, and it is what we must continue to build upon in the years ahead. Strong students and a strong faculty have produced academic excellence and intellectual excitement which in time have given Wellesley its place of prestige among educational institutions.

President Barbara Newell, 1974

Sundial, Tower Court

Science Center

Buildings on the rolling, peaceful Wellesley campus are generally of the Collegiate Gothic variety, and many of them are handsome specimens of that type. It is something of a shock, then, when one comes to the gleaming, machinelike Science Center standing across a wide open field. But the sense of shock does not last, partly because of the undeniable elegance of the form, and also the realization that this building actually fits in quite nicely with those around it. After all, its antecedents and theirs are, in some respects, to be found in the same sources. With respect to its most obvious image, the new building is much further removed from the sources than are those that found inspiration only in surface decoration. In terms of building theory and aesthetics, however, it may be a little closer to the true meaning of the Gothic originals.

David Morton in *Progressive Architecture*, March 1978

Jewett Arts Center

Buildings and groups should grow out of their sites and environment, not impose themselves on them, and...the great and beautiful features of hills, valleys, meadows, groves and winding roads should be preserved inviolate.

Ralph Adams Cram, "Report Upon a General Plan for Architectural Development," 1915

[Wellesley] that most delightful, that incredible girls' university, set in a broad park with a clubhouse among glades and trees.

H.G. Wells, 1905

Wellesley would not be Wellesley without an appreciation of beauty. It appeared in the earliest days when Mr. Durant built the building most of us have never seen, a building which emphasized "gracious living" as an essential in higher education. Surely a glance about us on this campus will convince anyone that that thread has never been dropped from the Wellesley pattern.

President Mildred H. McAfee, opening convocation, September 26, 1936

Opening Convocation, Hay Outdoor Theatre

"Spoonholder" on shore of Lake Waban

Wellesley is truly a place for all seasons of the mind and body and spirit — a wonderfully pastoral and serene background for rigorous intellectual exploration.

President Nannerl Keohane

All-College Picnic on Severance Green

4FT 8IN

Wellesley

The College is more than any group of people, faculty and students, gathered at any one time. It is the resultant power of the effort, the endeavor, the inspiration of all who have lived in it, and of those who shall live; a stream of life; a continuity of thought which has in it the elements of eternity.

President Caroline Hazard, 1909

"Fire and Water" bonfire by Lake Waban

TOWER COURT MIXER

Boston

Where, O where, are the grand old Seniors?
Safe now in the wide, wide world.
They've gone out from their Alma Mater,
Safe now in the wide, wide world.

Traditional Wellesley song

Wellesley

The Boston Marathon

1992
WELLESLEY
COLLEGE

1989

It is doubly a pleasure to me to come to these parts where I had spent four consecutively happy years of my student days, and where I had been imbued with the atmosphere of quiet gentility, of mutual consideration, of the inspiriting of personal integrity and of intellectual recherche and exchange of ideas and ideals so necessary to an enriched life....These happy times, in reminscence, were only possible within the purfled walls, enchanting woodlands, and spacious grounds prior to leaving Wellesley for the hard and often inhospitable world outside.

Madame Chiang Kai-Shek, address at Wellesley, December, 1965

Baccalaureate, Houghton Memorial Chapel

Previous page: Step singing in front of Houghton Memorial Chapel

FLOWER SUNDAY

Today the weather is rather obvious. Some people will wonder why Wellesley does not call off classes. It almost never has. As the minister yesterday told me, he did not bother to call to see if the service at Wellesley would be cancelled. "I know Wellesley," he said. "Wellesley would not stop for hell or high water."

President Margaret Clapp, chapel talk

Margaret Clapp Library

Rare Book Room, Margaret Clapp Library

Severance Hall dining room

We are not simple people here at Wellesley. We are intellectuals, many of us — that is, people who really enjoy the complexities of the thinking process, who really enjoy, not merely the adornment of the mind, but efforts to create and develop concepts.

President Margaret Clapp, chapel talk

I IV V I

Encyclopedia AMERICANA
ENCYCLOPÆDIA
BRITANNICA

The higher education of women is one of the great world battle cries for freedom, for right against might ... I believe that God's hand is in it; that it is one of the great ocean currents of Christian civilization; that He is calling to womanhood to come up higher, to prepare herself for great conflicts, for vast reforms in social life, for noblest usefulness.

Wellesley founder Henry Fowle Durant, in a sermon, 1877

Hoop rolling

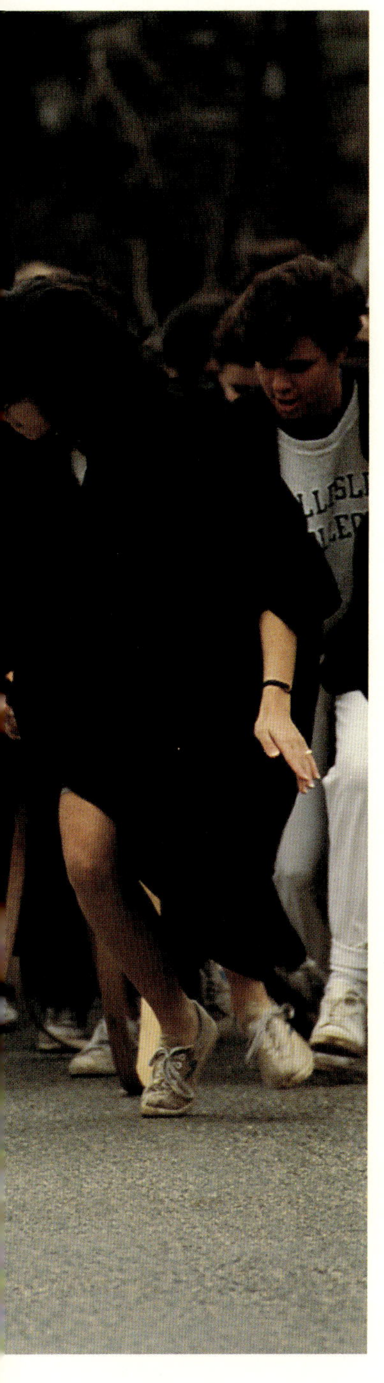

Commencement

1982
BRUT 1982
BRUT 1982
CHAMPAGNE
PERRIER-JOUËT
EPERNAY-FRANCE
BRUT
WELLESLEY COLLEGE

As we walk under the wonderful oaks of Wellesley today, see these great buildings and take a long look across beautiful Lake Waban, we naturally say to ourselves, "Here is the Wellesley world," and our thoughts are centered here. But I want you to realize, as I speak, that there is another Wellesley; that is worldwide and is made up of the hearts of those who have lived and worked and loved here, but who have been transplanted, not only over this country of ours, but far beyond— across seas and oceans...May we feel the power of their love and loyalty.

Mrs. Frances S. Williams, President of the Alumnae Association, speech October 19, 1911, at the inauguration of President Pendleton

COLLEGI WELLESLEIANI
Leah Marie Cook

A LOOK BACK AT

WELLESLEY COLLEGE

All photographs courtesy of the Wellesley College Archives.
Photo captions provided by Wilma R. Slaight.

College Hall housed all the students and faculty when Wellesley College opened in 1875. Designed by Hammatt Billings, College Hall extended for one-eighth of a mile on a hillside overlooking Lake Waban. Until Stone Hall, Music Hall and Simpson were built in 1880-81, College Hall housed all the College's classrooms and laboratories, library, chapel, gymnasium, and administrative and departmental offices.

Henry Fowle Durant (1822-1881). In 1854, Mr. Durant, a successful Harvard-educated Boston attorney, married his cousin, Pauline Fowle. They had two children, a daughter who died in infancy, and a son who died of diphtheria at the age of eight. The loss of their children deepened their commitment to their Christian faith, and prompted them to seek another use for their country estate. Mr. Durant was a trustee at Mt. Holyoke College, and Mrs. Durant had contributed generously to its library. At a time when the merits of higher education for women were being hotly debated, the Durants decided not just to open a college for women, but to found a college for women whose leaders and faculty were women.

College Hall fire. In the early hours of March 17, 1914, fire consumed College Hall, the administrative and emotional heart of the campus. Using skills learned through many fire drills, the 216 students and faculty living in the building escaped uninjured. Thankful that no lives were lost or injuries sustained, College officials faced a disaster of major proportions. Besides serving as a residence for 216 people, College Hall contained 28 classrooms, an assembly hall, a study hall, laboratories of the departments of geology, psychology, physics and zoology, administrative offices, offices of 20 departments (all except those of art, astronomy, chemistry, hygiene and music) and lunch and cloak rooms for non-resident faculty and students. Townspeople, alumnae and people from other colleges came to Wellesley's aid. When College reopened three weeks later (April 8) a temporary administration building had been built on the Chapel lawn, and other temporary arrangements for carrying on had been made. It took nearly two decades for the College to fully replace space and other facilities lost in the fire.

Student room, early 1880's.

Astronomy class, January 1917.

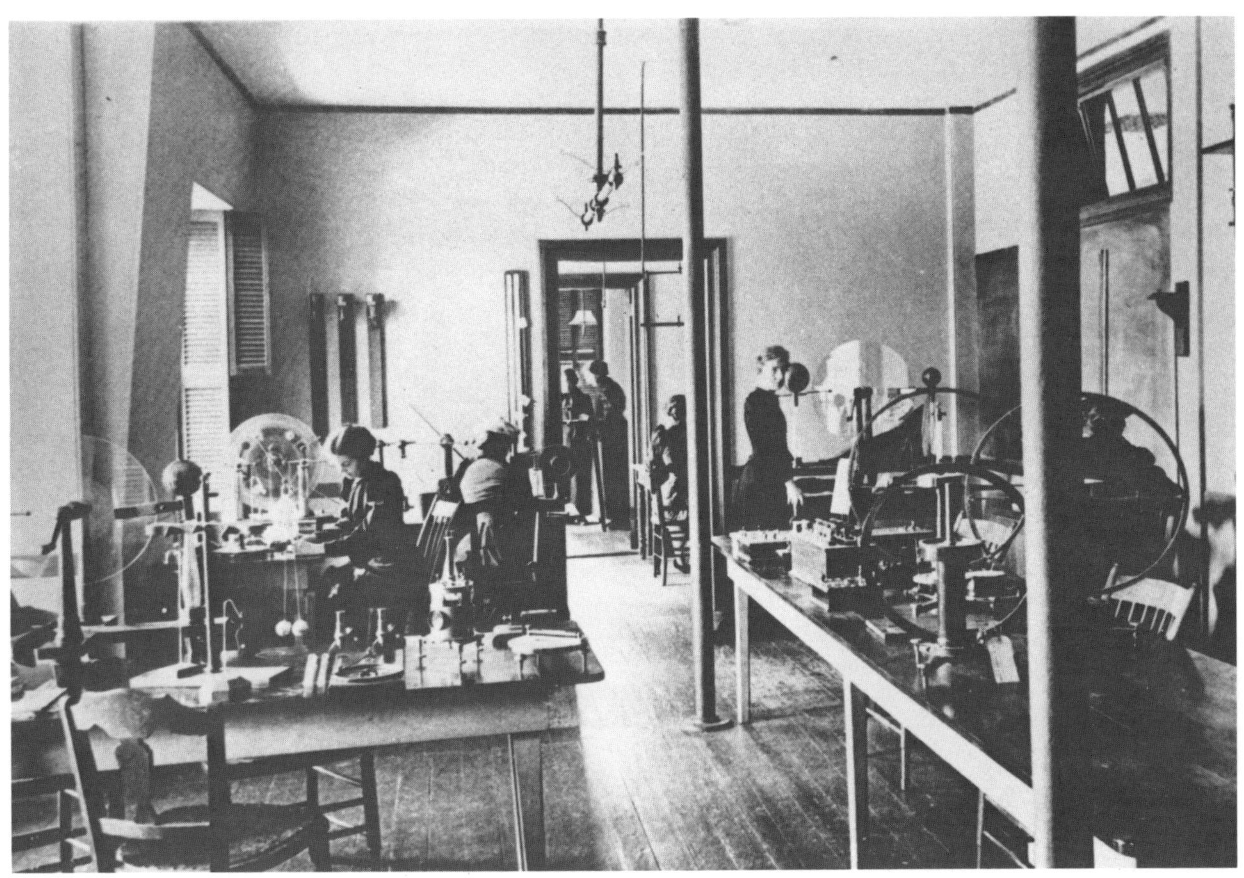

Physics Laboratory in College Hall. Teaching of science which includes students doing laboratory experiments has always been an important part of the liberal arts education at Wellesley. This was a fairly new idea when the college opened. The Physics laboratory at Wellesley was the second in the country (the first was at M.I.T.), and the first at a woman's college.

Library in College Hall. In 1910, four years before the College Hall fire, most library materials were moved into the new Library. Almost all of the collections which remained in College Hall, primarily a collection pertaining to North American Languages, were destroyed in the fire.

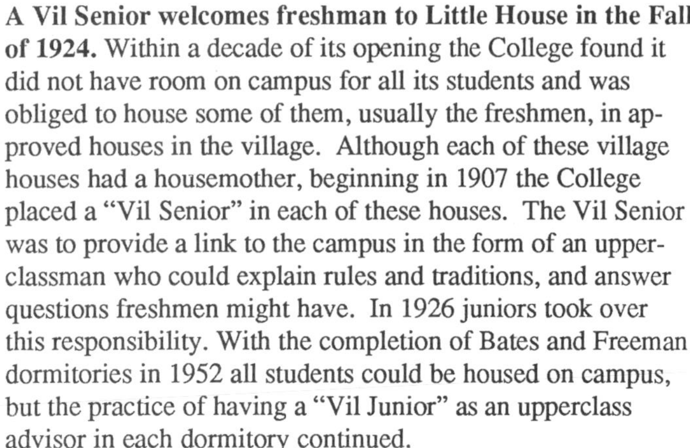

A Vil Senior welcomes freshman to Little House in the Fall of 1924. Within a decade of its opening the College found it did not have room on campus for all its students and was obliged to house some of them, usually the freshmen, in approved houses in the village. Although each of these village houses had a housemother, beginning in 1907 the College placed a "Vil Senior" in each of these houses. The Vil Senior was to provide a link to the campus in the form of an upperclassman who could explain rules and traditions, and answer questions freshmen might have. In 1926 juniors took over this responsibility. With the completion of Bates and Freeman dormitories in 1952 all students could be housed on campus, but the practice of having a "Vil Junior" as an upperclass advisor in each dormitory continued.

May Day, 1908. May Day featured the sophomore class forming the numerals of their sister class, the seniors.

Houghton Memorial Chapel. Designed by Heins and LaFarge, the architects of the Cathedral of St. John the Divine in New York City, the Chapel was completed in 1899. It was named in honor of William S. Houghton, who with his wife had served as Trustees of the College. It was first used for the inauguration of Caroline Hazard. This was also the first formal inauguration of a Wellesley President.

May Day, 1923. On May Day the students would dress up as children and engage in traditional May Day frolics.

Vacation. Students leaving for vacation, 1924.

Wellesley College from the air, circa 1921. This aerial photo shows the College beginning to rebuild after the College Hall fire. In the lower left corner the kitchen wing of College Hall, which did not burn in the fire, is seen next to Claflin and Tower Court, dormitories which in part replaced residential space lost in the fire. The H-shaped building in the foreground is the Library. Above it, next to the Farnsworth Art Building is Founders Hall, built to replace the space lost to humanities departments in the fire. In the lower right hand corner next to Billings Hall is the wooden U-shaped temporary administration building, the Hen Coop.

Basketball, early 1920's.

Float night. Class crews forming the "W" on Float Night, June, 1907. Float night, unlike early Tree Days, was open to the public. Float included boat races, crews forming a star and the "W", singing and pageantry on Lake Waban, and fireworks. After a hiatus for World War II, students tried to revive the tradition of Float, but fell victim to the weather. In 1949 after two floats in one generation of students were rained out, Float was abandoned. Crew races became part of Tree day.

Junior-Senior Field Hockey Game, Fall Field Day, 1930. Until the late 1960's Wellesley viewed the competitive spirit (and possible interference with course work) of intercollegiate sports as undesirable, and permitted only intramural sports, or informal sports with other women's colleges. At field day, held each spring and fall, class and dormitory teams competed against each other.

Mary Hemenway Hall. From the beginning Wellesley College recognized the need for its students to exercise, and required physical education as a part of the standard college course. In 1909 as part of the arrangement by which Wellesley College took over the Boston Normal School of Gymnastics a new gymnasium, Mary Hemenway Hall, was built. From 1909 until 1954 certificates and (after 1922) master's degrees were available from a graduate program in hygiene and physical education. In 1938 the Recreation Building added a pool and other sports facilities. Today, the needs of intercollegiate sports and the increased desire for recreational sports facilities on the part of students faculty and staff are met in the Sports Center which opened in 1985.

Hoop rolling. Above, Seniors ready for the start of hoop rolling, 1928. Hoop rolling, a Wellesley tradition since 1895, began as part of May Day celebrations. Seniors, in cap and gown, race with wooden hoops. Until recently it was said that the winner would be the first in her class to marry; now winning is said to presage success in her chosen field.

Archery. Wellesley women at the archery range, 1919.

Pendleton Hall, 1950's. Self-scheduled exams began in 1971. Wellesley students may take final exams at a time of their choosing during the examination period.

Founders Hall, Green Hall, and the Galen Stone Tower in 1931. Founders Hall, completed in 1919, replaced some of the classroom and departmental office space lost when College Hall was destroyed by fire in 1914. Permanent replacement of administrative office space had to wait until the completion of Hetty H. R. Green Hall in 1931. The Galen Stone Tower with its 30 bell carillion has become a College landmark.

Sage Hall, built 1926-31, housed the Botany and Zoology Departments. In 1974 facilities for these and other science departments were greatly improved with the construction of the Science Center and the adjacent Whitin Observatory.

Tree Day, 1936. Each class at Wellesley has a class tree. From 1877 to 1969 these trees were planted on Tree Day. Ceremonies included speeches, pageantry, and a procession of classes. Since 1970 the class tree has been planted, without the accompanying pageantry, as part of Sophomore Parents Weekend.

Women's Land Army Training Camp, 1918. As part of the war effort Wellesley allowed a contingent of the Women's Land Army of America to train on campus in the summer of 1918. The Camp Director, Edith Diehl, was a member of the Class of 1904. During the Second World War four groups of the Navy Supply Corps were trained at Wellesley.

Senior Prom, 1916. Until 1913, men were not permitted at Wellesley College dances.

"The Well." In 1939 part of the ballroom of Alumnae Hall was converted into a student center/snack bar named "The Well." During World War II this area was used as a mess hall by groups of the Navy Supply Corps training on campus. In 1970 Schneider College Center opened and "The Well" closed. Since 1974 the Wellesley Community Children's Center has occupied this space.

Step singing is a twentieth century Wellesley tradition. Students gather at the Chapel steps, juniors and seniors on the steps, first year students and sophomores on either side of the walk, to sing Wellesley and class songs, and to give the Wellesley cheer. At the last step singing of the year, the seniors relinquish their place of honor to the juniors.

Politics. Mock political campaign rally, 1948.

Hathaway House Bookshop, 1951. From 1927 until an on-campus bookstore opened in 1973 students bought their textbooks at the Hathaway House Bookshop adjacent to the campus in the village of Wellesley. Hathaway, founded in 1925 as a cooperative community bookstore for the village and the College, closed in 1979.

Claflin Hall

The **Main Reading Room** of the College Library was a preferred place for fireside study in the 1950's.